The Self-Care Planner

A WEEKLY GUIDE TO PRIORITIZE YOU

MEERA LESTER

Adams Media
New York   London   Toronto   Sydney   New Delhi

Adams Media
An Imprint of Simon & Schuster, Inc.
57 Littlefield Street
Avon, Massachusetts 02322

Copyright © 2019 by Simon & Schuster, Inc.

First Adams Media hardcover edition December 2019

ADAMS MEDIA and colophon are trademarks of Simon & Schuster.

For information about special discounts for bulk purchases, please contact Simon & Schuster Special Sales at 1-866-506-1949 or business@simonandschuster.com.

The Simon & Schuster Speakers Bureau can bring authors to your live event. For more information or to book an event contact the Simon & Schuster Speakers Bureau at 1-866-248-3049 or visit our website at www.simonspeakers.com.

Interior design by Colleen Cunningham
Hand lettering by Priscilla Yuen

Manufactured in China

10 9 8 7 6 5 4 3 2 1

Library of Congress Cataloging-in-Publication Data has been applied for.

ISBN 978-1-5072-1164-9
ISBN 978-1-5072-1165-6 (ebook)

Introduction

Do you struggle to find peaceful moments during your day?
Is it difficult to make time to exercise?
Do you wish you could focus more on your spiritual well-being?

We all know self-care is something we should do, but it's always the first thing we neglect. *The Self-Care Planner* empowers you to give yourself the priority you deserve—right at the top of your to-do list.

When you carve out moments during your day to focus on what you love about life, let go of guilt, and give positive thinking and acts of self-compassion precedence, your busy life becomes easier to manage. You recharge more quickly and, more importantly, protect your physical, mental, and emotional health.

You are a multidimensional being, so your self-care should reflect that—catering to your intellectual, emotional, physical, spiritual, and social needs. With *The Self-Care Planner*, it is easier than ever to enrich every month, week, and day of your life with meaningful, intentional self-care. There's no better time to get started than right now.

What Is an Intention?

An intention is something you desire to manifest into your life. More like a resolution than a wish, an intention could take the form of a guiding principle you want to live by. Setting an intention will require some forethought and planning, as well as the commitment to take actions to bring that intention into reality.

Practitioners of the ancient, universal Law of Attraction advocate declaring your intention and then reinforcing it with actions, affirmations, and visualizations. Your self-care journal will aid you in those endeavors because you can write down, keep track of, and create imagery in the form of notes to yourself and affirming statements.

When setting a self-care intention, specificity is key. Instead of proclaiming, "I want to get fit," refine your statement to something like, "I intend to lose three pounds this month through dance exercise." And instead of declaring, "I am going to get good at yoga," clarify with a statement about precisely how you intend to improve. "I intend to do a five-asana hatha yoga sequence every morning."

The more specific your statement of intention is, the more precise your road map will be for making your plan a reality. Perhaps you intend to drop three pounds, and you will do it through dance exercise. You can then ask yourself, "What actions could I take to ensure that this intention comes true?" You might start looking through community catalogs of adult classes, park and recreation programs, ballroom dancing clubs, and other avenues offering dance.

Since your overarching intention is to lose weight, you will want to consider all the ways to achieve that endeavor by setting smaller milestone goals—reducing calories, cutting out unhealthy snacks, and drinking enough water, for example. If your schedule is hectic and you rely on fast food meals, you might decide to eat fewer of those and more Buddha bowls with ancient grains, healthy fats, seeds and nuts, lean proteins, and fresh vegetables.

You could proclaim the intention to cut out two fast food meals each week to benefit your body.

Another intention might be to shift your pattern of eating from quickly devouring your food to eating more mindfully. Keep your thoughts focused on why you eat what you eat. Pay attention to the process you go through to prepare and consume each meal.

Finally, you might also consider stating an intention for your spirit. For example, you might meditate on what nourishes your inner spiritual life. Is it the sustenance you receive while sitting in meditation in a relaxed state of alertness? If so, declare a food-for-the-soul intention.

How to Use This Book

This self-care planner is designed as a powerful tool to honor your spiritual, mental, and physical needs. In the following pages, you'll find the following for every month:

- **A blank calendar page**, so that you can begin at any time of the year. Fill in the dates according to when you begin.

WED	TH	FRI
1 /	2 /	3 /
Yoga @5	AM Meditation	Hike with Mom ☺ 7 AM
	Book club @8	

- **This Month's Focus**, a particular theme for you to direct your energy toward. These universal themes are shared by people from all walks of life. You'll quickly discover how easy it is to start working on your goals, intentions, and activities because you can begin at any point of the year, in any year. Record your Self-Care Intentions for the Month using the monthly self-care focus as your guide. Be inspired by the quotes within.

- **Five weekly pages.** Stay focused by trying the weekly self-care tips for body, mind, and spirit. Use your Self-Care Intentions for the Week as a place to record your smaller milestone goals.

The planner will get you inspired. Use it to set intentions; establish goals; create action lists; keep track of progress; and even compose deep, reflective journaling about your self-care practices. Creating a healthier, happier, and more successful life is within reach. Everything starts in your mind with resolve and intention and expectation.

Self-care isn't selfish. It's all about personal transformation through acts of self-compassion. When you integrate self-care practices into your busy schedule, you are more confident, effective, and productive. Self-esteem and positivity increase. You reflect the healthy being of light and love that is you—powerful and authentic—from the inside out. It is self-care planning and action that take you there, and this planner is the tool that makes it easier than ever to accomplish your goals. Inspiration, accountability, and execution all in one, *The Self-Care Planner* is the simplest way to take care of your whole being the way you truly deserve.

Instill Calm

SUN	MON	TUES	
/	/	/	
/	/	/	
/	/	/	
/	/	/	
/	/	/	

"Breathing in, I calm body and mind. Breathing out, I smile. Dwelling in the present moment I know this is the only moment."

—Thich Nhat Hanh, Vietnamese Zen Buddhist master

WED	TH	FRI	SAT
/	/	/	/
/	/	/	/
/	/	/	/
/	/	/	/
/	/	/	/

Instill Calm

When you have to tackle something difficult, try to slow the cycles of your breath to instill calm. Slow, rhythmic breathing provides your brain with more oxygen. You feel mentally alert and clearheaded. Instead of feeling overwhelmed and doubting your ability to rise to the challenge, stop and center yourself. Take a few moments to sit quietly, breathe slowly, and invite calmness to permeate your being. Within the circle of your solitude is everything you need.

My Self-Care Intentions for the Month

_____

_____

_____

_____

_____

_____

_____

_____

month 1

"Your calm mind is the ultimate weapon against your challenges. So relax."

—Bryant McGill, American author

Notes

BODY Awaken Your Center of Power

Halfway between your heart and belly button is your solar plexus. Activate this acupressure point to increase self-confidence and calm anxiety. Push your thumb against the spot. Hold for one minute to trigger healing energy. Release, relax, and repeat.

MIND Slow the Brain's Activity

The waking mind generates brain-wave frequencies that range between thirteen and thirty cycles per second (cps). Those frequencies drop to eight to thirteen cps during meditation when your heart rate and respirations slow. As the mind and body align, calmness prevails. Practice a soothing meditation first thing in the morning to set the tone for your day.

SPIRIT Soothe Your Spirit

Mental and physical turbulences often cause a restless spirit. But when you can surrender to a higher power, releasing expectations and the desire to control particular outcomes, your spirit settles into peaceful acceptance. In times of trouble, recognize what you can control and what is beyond your grasp. Doing so will relieve your mind of unnecessary worry.

My Self-Care Intentions for the Week

BODY ....

MIND ....

SPIRIT ....

Week of   /   /

As you schedule your week, keep your self-care intentions in mind.

Sunday

Monday

Tuesday

Wednesday

Thursday

Friday

Saturday

How did I do?

....

....

....

BODY Recite a Calming Mantra

When life gets chaotic, find a mantra to recite that makes you feel in control and calm, such as "Peace be with me and also with you." Repeating the mantra during a difficult or chaotic time can be your refuge.

MIND Believe Anything Is Possible

Give your mind free rein to embrace all sorts of possibilities that you might have previously dismissed. A century ago, walking on the moon would have been a fantasy beyond the scope of possibility. Today, it's an undisputed accomplishment. When you feel yourself thinking, "That's impossible!" replace the sentiment with, "Wouldn't it be wonderful if...?" or "It will be amazing *when*..." to remind yourself of what can be achieved.

SPIRIT Beckon Divine Assistance

The stresses of living in the modern world might occasionally knock you off-balance, sapping your sanity, strength, and stamina. When you feel inward chaos, tap your belief in a higher power to restore your sense of balance. Take a moment to ask the Universe for guidance, and make your soul receptive to a response.

My Self-Care Intentions for the Week

BODY ....

MIND ....

SPIRIT ....

week 2

month 1

Week of   /   /

As you schedule your week, keep your self-care intentions in mind.

Sunday

Monday

Tuesday

Wednesday

Thursday

Friday

Saturday

How did I do?

....

....

....

BODY Sink Into a Scented Bath

The ancient Greek physician Hippocrates recommended taking an aromatic bath every day to improve health. The key to washing away stress is to relax your whole being. Luxuriating in a bath can help you feel revitalized and restored.

MIND Install a Tabletop Fountain

There's nothing like sitting near a babbling brook or waterfall to instill calm. Achieve a similar benefit by sitting in a chair near a tabletop fountain. Close your eyes. Relax your muscles. Listen to the sound of running water washing away your worry.

SPIRIT Wear Amethyst

Crystal workers believe that amethyst emits gentle, relaxing energies. Because it is regarded as a protective and healing stone, crystal therapies use amethyst to aid in the treatment of insomnia and night terrors, as well as to balance the crown chakra.

week 3

month 1

My Self-Care Intentions for the Week

BODY ....

MIND ....

SPIRIT ....

Week of   /   /

As you schedule your week, keep your self-care intentions in mind.

Sunday

Monday

Tuesday

Wednesday

Thursday

Friday

Saturday

How did I do?

....

....

....

BODY Clear the Clutter

Few things are as unsettling as messy spaces in your home or at work. Clearing these spaces so they are organized, efficient, and clean can restore your sense of calm. Tackle the work in increments and take frequent breaks.

MIND Visualize Feeling Calm

To regain a sense of calm, sit and close your eyes to shut out any visual input. Place your fingertips against your ears to shut out sound. Breathe quietly and slowly. Visualize calmness descending over you like a diaphanous veil.

SPIRIT Burn Sage

Burning sage (also called smudging) is an ancient ritual associated with the spiritual traditions of Native Americans. Choose white prairie sage. It repels insects and has antimicrobial and antibacterial properties. It's believed to dispel negative energies and exert a calming effect.

week 4

month 1

My Self-Care Intentions for the Week

BODY ....

MIND ....

SPIRIT ....

Week of   /   /

As you schedule your week, keep your self-care intentions in mind.

Sunday

Monday

Tuesday

Wednesday

Thursday

Friday

Saturday

How did I do?

....

....

....

BODY Get Grounded with the Earth Star Chakra

Many people are familiar with the seven chakras, or energy centers, in our bodies, but some disciplines recognize more chakras. The earth star chakra is below your feet and can be activated simply by placing your bare feet against the earth. To feel more grounded and calm, place hematite or smoky quartz around your feet.

MIND Mentally Tune to Your Causal Chakra

The shimmering white causal chakra (three to four inches above the crown chakra) helps you filter out the noise of life. Blue kyanite (in sedimentary rock) facilitates the shift to tranquility when it is placed at the back of your head. Lie on your back in Corpse Pose with a small, smooth piece of kyanite positioned at the base of your skull to align and rebalance your chakras.

SPIRIT Activate the Gateway Chakra

Another lesser-known chakra is the stellar gateway chakra, located above the head. This energy center is the conduit between your spirit and the Source of your being. Meditate on this chakra to gain balance and calm as you are guided to wisdom.

My Self-Care Intentions for the Week

BODY ....

MIND ....

SPIRIT ....

Week of   /   /

As you schedule your week, keep your self-care intentions in mind.

Sunday

Monday

Tuesday

Wednesday

Thursday

Friday

Saturday

How did I do?

....

....

....

Move Mindfully

SUN	MON	TUES
/	/	/
/	/	/
/	/	/
/	/	/
/	/	/

"All motion is cyclic. It circulates to the limits of its possibilities and then returns to its starting point."

—Robert Collier, American motivational author

WED	TH	FRI	SAT
/	/	/	/
/	/	/	/
/	/	/	/
/	/	/	/
/	/	/	/

Move Mindfully

In ancient Greece, the physician Hippocrates advocated exercise for mind-body balance. In India, people practiced yoga. In China, tai chi became popular. Yoga movements generate within you an optimum state of relaxed alertness, while tai chi links your mind with body and breath to stimulate the flow of chi (powerful life energy) for optimum health. This month's self-care activities emphasize mindful movement—not militant, but gentle—according to your body's own wisdom of what feels right.

My Self-Care Intentions for the Month

_____

_____

_____

_____

_____

_____

_____

_____

month 2

"All motion is cyclic. It circulates to the limits of its possibilities and then returns to its starting point."

—Robert Collier, American motivational author

WED	TH	FRI	SAT
/	/	/	/
/	/	/	/
/	/	/	/
/	/	/	/
/	/	/	/

Move Mindfully

In ancient Greece, the physician Hippocrates advocated exercise for mind-body balance. In India, people practiced yoga. In China, tai chi became popular. Yoga movements generate within you an optimum state of relaxed alertness, while tai chi links your mind with body and breath to stimulate the flow of chi (powerful life energy) for optimum health. This month's self-care activities emphasize mindful movement—not militant, but gentle—according to your body's own wisdom of what feels right.

My Self-Care Intentions for the Month

_____

_____

_____

_____

_____

_____

_____

_____

month 2

"Only love is motion and rest in one."

—Rabindranath Tagore, Indian poet, playwright, and essayist

Notes

BODY Balance Opposing Energies

Chinese medicine identifies two types of energy—yin and yang—that power your body. Rest to experience yin. Run to know yang. These opposing energies are perpetually moving, influencing each other. Strive for balance by practicing resting and active self-care.

MIND Contemplate Your Inner "Male" and "Female"

Carl Jung theorized that we have an inner male (*animus*) and female (*anima*) composing our collective unconscious. Tap into your inner male/female energies for motivation to get up and go. If you are female, your animus is reflected in the rational, problem-solving, masculine aspects of your psyche, while your anima shines forth in your soulful, empathetic, and nurturing feminine qualities.

SPIRIT Be Guided by the Yin and Yang Symbol

Picture a circle, half black and half white. Each side contains a dot of the opposing side's color to reflect Creation's opposing energies interacting harmoniously. Use the symbol to guide your spirit by meditating on the feminine yin (dark) side of the symbol and then on the masculine yang (light) side. Too much yang can agitate your energy, and too much yin can result in low vitality. Balanced energies create a peaceful spirit.

My Self-Care Intentions for the Week

BODY ....

MIND ....

SPIRIT ....

week 1

month 2

Week of   /   /

As you schedule your week, keep your self-care intentions in mind.

Sunday

Monday

Tuesday

Wednesday

Thursday

Friday

Saturday

How did I do?

....

....

....

BODY Take a Mindful Stroll

Stand. Inhale (your belly should rise to the count of five) and exhale. How does your body feel? Breathe and walk. Focus on your body's balance, the movement of air in and out of your lungs, and your heel-to-toe rhythm.

MIND Focus Your Mind on the Breath

Mindful movements during exercise can link thinking to breathing. During your self-care regimen, if your mental awareness shifts to other sensory input in your environment, bring it back into the quiet groove that feels like a meditative practice.

SPIRIT Shift Your Vibe, Lift Your Spirit

When you slip into a negative mood like anger because honking cars are disturbing your morning walk to the park, remember that change happens in every moment. Remind yourself that anger can be momentary. Breathe away tension. Shift your vibe.

My Self-Care Intentions for the Week

BODY ....

MIND ....

SPIRIT ....

Week of   /   /

As you schedule your week, keep your self-care intentions in mind.

Sunday

Monday

Tuesday

Wednesday

Thursday

Friday

Saturday

How did I do?

....

....

....

BODY Dive Deeply Into Nature

Swim, hike, camp, or dance out in nature to gain powerful, positive, and healing effects throughout your whole being. Let nature work her magic on you. Make your movements meditative by placing a mindful focus on the multisensory connections nature offers.

MIND Mind the Moment

Thoughts are like clouds; they can gather and darken or pull apart and reflect the bright sky. Your thoughts might dwell on the past or worry about the future. Fleeting thoughts neither define nor control you. For self-care, focus on the present.

SPIRIT Be Open to Divine Insight

Balance sessions of mindful movements with those of mental quiet. Sit peacefully with eyes closed and breathing relaxed. Turn your inward gaze gently upward (don't strain). Opening yourself to Divine guidance will help you become a more self-caring and compassionate being.

month 2   week 3

My Self-Care Intentions for the Week

BODY ....

MIND ....

SPIRIT ....

Week of   /   /

As you schedule your week, keep your self-care intentions in mind.

Sunday

Monday

Tuesday

Wednesday

Thursday

Friday

Saturday

How did I do?

....

....

....

BODY Use Mindfulness with Weightlifting

You begin to lose muscle mass at age thirty. You can replace it by lifting weights a few times each week. Weightlifting can guard against your getting osteoporosis. Focus on each muscle (or group) with mindfulness as you work out.

MIND Zap Depression with Exercise

Clinical trials examining the relationship between exercise and mood have shown that exercise might be as effective in treating depression as psychotherapy. Stimulate circulation and increase blood flow to every area of your body and brain by making exercise a regular self-care activity.

SPIRIT Cultivate Detachment

Learn to disengage from stressful situations. Develop objectivity. Realize that difficult emotions do not have to dictate your movement into action. Detachment is caring in a deep way for your spirit so that you allow its wisdom to guide you.

week 4

month 2

My Self-Care Intentions for the Week

BODY ....

MIND ....

SPIRIT ....

Week of   /   /

As you schedule your week, keep your self-care intentions in mind.

Sunday

Monday

Tuesday

Wednesday

Thursday

Friday

Saturday

How did I do?

....

....

....

BODY Be Mindful During Vigorous Workouts Too

Moving with mindfulness doesn't apply to only easy movements. Observe your exercise as the experience unfolds. Tune in to how your body is handling it, without being judgmental. Focus on what you are doing, evaluate how your body feels, and adjust.

MIND Work Out Your Wellness Needs

To meet all of your physical, emotional, and psychological needs every day, ask yourself what you need to maintain a happy mood, a healthy body, and a childlike sense of wonder and curiosity. Prioritize your new to-do items.

SPIRIT Be Kind to Your Musculoskeletal System

Your competitive spirit could drive you to push your body to its limits. Enjoy your sport, fitness, and competition. Warm up muscles before exercise and cool down afterward. Use mindfulness to uplift your body rather than pushing it into injury.

month 2   week 5

My Self-Care Intentions for the Week

BODY ....

MIND ....

SPIRIT ....

Week of   /   /

As you schedule your week, keep your self-care intentions in mind.

Sunday

Monday

Tuesday

Wednesday

Thursday

Friday

Saturday

How did I do?

....

....

....

Connect with Nature

SUN	MON	TUES
/	/	/
/	/	/
/	/	/
/	/	/
/	/	/

"Reading about nature is fine, but if a person walks in the woods and listens carefully, he can learn more than what is in books."

—George Washington Carver, American agricultural scientist and inventor

WED	TH	FRI	SAT
/	/	/	/
/	/	/	/
/	/	/	/
/	/	/	/
/	/	/	/

Connect with Nature

Scientific studies have shown numerous health benefits from interacting with nature, including improved memory, decreased blood pressure and heart rate, and lowered levels of the stress hormone cortisol. Take a walk in the woods to banish brain fatigue. Linger among plants and trees in a woodland or meadow to ease anxiety and depression. Think of your self-care activities in the wild as nature therapy.

My Self-Care Intentions for the Month

_____

_____

_____

_____

_____

_____

_____

_____

month 3

"One touch of nature makes the whole world kin."

—William Shakespeare, English playwright

Notes

BODY Walk on the Wild Side

Take a jaunt into the woods to refresh, relax, and reenergize. Exercising in a natural environment increases your brain's endorphins, the "feel good" chemicals. The sun's vitamin D helps ease depression. Let nature nourish you as she does all her kin.

MIND Summon Your Inner Gardener

To garden is to nurture. Precisely because caring for plants is a solitary activity, your mind moves from anxiety and worry to serenity. Let your mind wrap around the notion of how the growth of a tree might exemplify endurance, patience, stability, and groundedness.

SPIRIT Meditate Beneath a Tree

Trees have spiritual significance in many traditions. The ash, hawthorn, and oak composed the Celts' sacred trilogy. Buddha attained enlightenment beneath a bodhi tree. Sit under a tree. Sense its energy rising from taproot to canopy. Feel your spirit soar.

week 1

month 3

My Self-Care Intentions for the Week

BODY ....

MIND ....

SPIRIT ....

Week of   /   /

As you schedule your week, keep your self-care intentions in mind.

Sunday

Monday

Tuesday

Wednesday

Thursday

Friday

Saturday

How did I do?

....

....

....

BODY Plant an Herb Garden

Herbs have been an important part of medical practice since ancient times. The Ebers Papyrus of herbal knowledge dates to 1550 B.C. and contains roughly seven hundred magical formulas and medicinal folk remedies used by the ancient Egyptians. Practice self-care by planting herbs for healthy eating and wellness.

MIND Use Herbs to Boost Mental Tasks

Water hyssop has been used in India for thousands of years to regenerate neural tissues and thwart brain aging. Traditional Chinese medicine credits ginkgo biloba with enhancing concentration and memory (especially when combined with ginseng). Parsley also boosts brain power. Give herbs a role in your self-care.

SPIRIT Try Dry Herbs for Spiritual Protection

In some cultures, herbs such as garlic, basil, fennel, and oregano are believed to protect against and deter dark forces. To tap into the spiritual protective properties of these herbs, dry them and insert them into a pouch to hang on your front door.

My Self-Care Intentions for the Week

BODY ....

MIND ....

SPIRIT ....

week 2

month 3

Week of   /   /

As you schedule your week, keep your self-care intentions in mind.

Sunday

Monday

Tuesday

Wednesday

Thursday

Friday

Saturday

How did I do?

....

....

....

BODY Make and Hang a Birdfeeder

You can make a birdfeeder out of almost anything; for example, a pottery saucer. Drill three equally spaced holes and loop wire through them. Add seeds, hang, and check daily. Welcome the birds. Let their songs lift your spirit.

MIND Enjoy Peace of Mind

Many avian species are disappearing in what is being called the sixth mass extinction. Gain peace of mind by assisting in saving a species. Learn about the habits and needs of your area's native birds. Consider how you might create a habitat for an endangered species.

SPIRIT Craft an Amulet from Nature Discoveries

If you come across a bird feather while in the woods, use it and other objects found in nature to create an amulet for spiritual well-being. Some cultures believe that bird feathers symbolize ascension, and spiritualists say that when angels are near, feathers appear.

week 3

month 3

My Self-Care Intentions for the Week

BODY ....

MIND ....

SPIRIT ....

Week of   /   /

As you schedule your week, keep your self-care intentions in mind.

Sunday

Monday

Tuesday

Wednesday

Thursday

Friday

Saturday

How did I do?

....

....

....

BODY Try Hops for Restful Sleep

A millennium ago, English brewers discovered that hops (flowers of the hop plant) functioned as a stability agent in beer. Today, science has shown that hops contain sedative properties. Consider adding hops tea to your bedtime self-care practice to help with insomnia.

MIND Deepen Your Emotional Connection to Nature

Ecology and psychology are linked in a single term—*eco-psychology*. The term encapsulates the premise that culture shapes modern minds, whereas evolution in the natural world shapes and informs the deep mind structure. To access your deep mind, surround yourself with nature.

SPIRIT Decipher Your Nature Dreams

Dreaming of nature? Nature symbolism might suggest freedom or that you need to break free from something. Keep a dream journal. Write, decipher, and analyze your dreamtime forays. Learn what your spirit might be communicating through nature symbols.

My Self-Care Intentions for the Week

BODY ....

MIND ....

SPIRIT ....

week 4

month 3

Week of   /   /

As you schedule your week, keep your self-care intentions in mind.

Sunday

Monday

Tuesday

Wednesday

Thursday

Friday

Saturday

How did I do?

....

....

....

BODY Taste Nature's Sweetness

Participate in a local honey-tasting event. Produced by honeybees, honey contains antioxidants and curbs the appetite. Two teaspoons daily may help fight cell damage. Some honey types inhibit cancer cell growth in mice.

MIND Reflect On How to Help the Bees

Increase your understanding of how important bees are to the natural world. Plant a pollinator garden (even in a pot) as a self-care act that benefits you and them. Consider other ways you might assist the beleaguered bees.

SPIRIT Meditate On Bee Symbolism

To the ancient Druids, the bee symbolized the sun, the Goddess, family, and celebration. The Celts believed bees carried messages between the worlds—to paradise and back. Consider: what self-care messages might the bees transport from the invisible world to you?

week 5

month 3

My Self-Care Intentions for the Week

BODY ....

MIND ....

SPIRIT ....

Week of   /   /

As you schedule your week, keep your self-care intentions in mind.

Sunday

Monday

Tuesday

Wednesday

Thursday

Friday

Saturday

How did I do?

Manifest Peace and Kindness

SUN	MON	TUES
/	/	/
/	/	/
/	/	/
/	/	/
/	/	/

month 4

"Serenity is not freedom from the storm, but peace amid the storm."

—Anonymous

WED	TH	FRI	SAT
/	/	/	/
/	/	/	/
/	/	/	/
/	/	/	/
/	/	/	/

Manifest Peace and Kindness

American writer and humorist Mark Twain opined that kindness is "the language the deaf can hear and the blind can see." The point he was making is that language isn't needed where peace and kindness prevail. Showing kindness to others yields positive benefits to the giver. Altruistic acts boost levels of the "feel good" neurotransmitter serotonin and the endorphins your body normally releases during exercise (a phenomenon known as "helper's high").

My Self-Care Intentions for the Month

_____

_____

_____

_____

_____

_____

_____

_____

_____

month 4

"You must be the change you want to see in the world."

—Mohandas K. Gandhi, Indian nonviolent social activist, lawyer, and spiritual leader

Notes

This Week's Tips to Manifest Peace and Kindness

BODY Engage in Acts of Kindness

Offer smiles and silent blessings to everyone you meet. Donate time at an animal shelter, work at a hospice, or donate blood to save a life. Your gift of kindness to another is a self-care act that bestows benefits of well-being on you.

MIND Think Kind, Compassionate, and Peaceful Thoughts

The ancient universal Law of Attraction advocates positive thinking to bring powerful blessings into your life. Negative thoughts pollute the mind. They can generate harmful effects on your psyche. Instead, seed your life with positive thoughts to bless yourself and others.

SPIRIT Soothe Your Spirit

Be kind to yourself. Close your eyes, sit quietly, and chant the sacred "Aum" (or "Om") mantra, which originated in the Hindu Vedic tradition. Slowly utter the sounds without breaking them as you end with *m-m-m*. Relax into peace.

week 1

month 4

My Self-Care Intentions for the Week

BODY ....

MIND ....

SPIRIT ....

Week of   /   /

As you schedule your week, keep your self-care intentions in mind.

Sunday

Monday

Tuesday

Wednesday

Thursday

Friday

Saturday

How did I do?

....

....

....

BODY Give the Gift of Body Strength

Schedule a visit to someone who is ill or has limited mobility. Offer to clean a cupboard. Clip the roses. Make tea. See the gift of your physical ability and an hour of your time as compassion toward your friend, as well as self-care for you.

MIND Shift the Paradigm to Solve Conflicts

The Buddha, Gandhi, Dr. Martin Luther King, and Nelson Mandela are spiritual exemplars who took nonviolent approaches to conflict resolution. Sometimes just one person can shift the paradigm to peacefully solve conflicts at home or in the world. Remain silent and walk away when an argument erupts between you and someone else. One person can't argue if the other person has left.

SPIRIT Formulate a Peaceful Affirmation

Discord quickly destroys serenity, making peace hard to hold on to despite your best effort. To tamp down feelings of anxiousness from episodes of disharmony, include in your self-care regimen an affirmation such as "I am holding on to inner peace."

My Self-Care Intentions for the Week

BODY ....

MIND ....

SPIRIT ....

month 4   week 2

Week of   /   /

As you schedule your week, keep your self-care intentions in mind.

Sunday

Monday

Tuesday

Wednesday

Thursday

Friday

Saturday

How did I do?

....

....

....

This Week's Tips to Manifest Peace and Kindness

BODY Let Scent Call Forth Inner Peace

Try aromatherapy using oils especially associated with instilling peace—ylang-ylang for peaceful balance, bergamot for hormone balancing, or lemon for that deep sense of well-being. Sprinkle a few drops onto a cotton ball to sniff throughout your day.

MIND Imagine Your Kindness Flowing Back to You

There is truth in the old adage that what you send out returns to you. When you imagine what you'd like to manifest, your imagination stimulates the same neurological network as the actual experience. Your prefrontal cortex takes your desire as an instruction to create it.

SPIRIT Let the Wisdom of a Spiritual Teacher Guide You

Peace activist and Zen master Thich Nhat Hanh teaches that we "have to walk in a way that we only print peace and serenity on the Earth. Walk as if you are kissing the Earth with your feet." Let his words sink into your spirit.

My Self-Care Intentions for the Week

BODY ....

MIND ....

SPIRIT ....

Week of   /   /

As you schedule your week, keep your self-care intentions in mind.

Sunday

Monday

Tuesday

Wednesday

Thursday

Friday

Saturday

How did I do?

....

....

....

BODY Eat Five Fruits and Vegetables Daily

Eating a healthy diet is an act of kindness toward your body. Nutritious foods are just as easy to eat as ones that simply satisfy your oral gratification needs. Make eating well part of your self-care this week.

MIND Silence Your Self-Critic

Why beat up or berate yourself? What purpose does that serve? It is so much better to show kindness to yourself by tuning out that harsh inner taskmaster. Change your vulnerability to strength by offering words of praise instead.

SPIRIT Turn Away from the News

Turn off the TV, cell phone, and electronic devices. Take a break from the news, which is often packed with negative messages. It's easier to tune in to your angels, spirit guides, a higher power, and your higher self when inner peace prevails.

week 4

month 4

My Self-Care Intentions for the Week

BODY ....

MIND ....

SPIRIT ....

Week of   /   /

As you schedule your week, keep your self-care intentions in mind.

Sunday

Monday

Tuesday

Wednesday

Thursday

Friday

Saturday

How did I do?

BODY Give Yourself Permission to Say No

If agreeing to something means your stress level is going to skyrocket, then politely decline. It isn't your job to please everyone. Accommodating everyone else's needs makes it difficult to attend to your own. Appropriate refusals can be acts of self-kindness.

MIND Let Go of Old Hurts

Do your thoughts keep cycling through past mistakes and hurts that happened long ago? You have the power in every moment to change directions, to forgive yourself and release the guilt. Stop re-treading old ground. Replace old hurts with thoughts of loving-kindness.

SPIRIT Surrender to Truth

It requires a lot of mental and emotional energy to hold old hurts, anger, and negative memories inside. A therapy session with a professional might help you gain perspective and learn how to let go. Let the light in to give your spirit peace.

month 4 week 5

My Self-Care Intentions for the Week

BODY ....

MIND ....

SPIRIT ....

Week of   /   /

As you schedule your week, keep your self-care intentions in mind.

Sunday

Monday

Tuesday

Wednesday

Thursday

Friday

Saturday

How did I do?

....

....

....

Honor Your Body

SUN	MON	TUES
/	/	/
/	/	/
/	/	/
/	/	/
/	/	/

"Forget not that the earth delights to feel your bare feet and the winds long to play with your hair."

—Kahlil Gibran, Lebanese-American author and poet

WED	TH	FRI	SAT
/	/	/	/
/	/	/	/
/	/	/	/
/	/	/	/
/	/	/	/

Honor Your Body

Cultivate a positive attitude toward your beautiful body. After all, it serves you throughout your life and carries you forward to achieve your dreams. Respect and honor your body and give it the care it needs. Start blessing your food, eating more healthfully and mindfully, stretching daily, making time for exercise, hydrating, de-stressing, and getting enough sleep. Integrate these self-care practices and notice the difference in how you think and feel about your extraordinary body.

My Self-Care Intentions for the Month

_____

_____

_____

_____

_____

_____

_____

_____

_____

month 5

"The body achieves what the mind believes."

—Anonymous

Notes

_____

_____

_____

_____

_____

_____

_____

_____

_____

_____

_____

_____

_____

BODY Achieve a Healthy and Beautiful Body Now

Release ideas of how you think others see your body. With robust health and emotional well-being comes a positive self-image. Proper care and feeding of your body can make it the most beautiful and healthy it can be.

MIND Engage in Body Mindfulness at Mealtimes

Easy self-care tips for weight loss include eating slowly, savoring each bite, and practicing mindfulness with each mouthful. Think about the taste and texture of the food and how the right foods translate to radiant skin and brighter eyes.

SPIRIT Give Thanks for Healthy Food on Your Plate

Make a mealtime ritual of gratitude for the plants, animals, and people that make possible the food on your plate. When you think peaceful, positive, and grateful thoughts while consuming a meal, you assume a beautiful generosity of spirit toward all beings.

week 1

month 5

My Self-Care Intentions for the Week

BODY ....

MIND ....

SPIRIT ....

Week of   /   /

As you schedule your week, keep your self-care intentions in mind.

Sunday

Monday

Tuesday

Wednesday

Thursday

Friday

Saturday

How did I do?

....

....

....

BODY Get an Acupressure Massage

Acupressure is a holistic healing modality practiced for thousands of years in China. For self-care, schedule a massage with an acupressure therapist. Pressure is applied along your body's energy pathways to relieve pain and generate wellness. Isn't it time for a tune-up?

MIND Correct Your Thinking about Your Body

Studies show that your feelings, beliefs, and attitudes—whether positive or negative—influence your biological function. Root out negative thinking about your body's appearance. Replace your tendency to be self-critical with acknowledgment of how beautiful you are, inside and out. The next time you think, "My fat calves extend from thunder thighs," change the thought to, "Look how far my strong legs and thighs have taken me."

SPIRIT Tap the Power of the Tulsi Plant

Invigorate and rejuvenate your spirit with a cup of tulsi tea. In Ayurveda (traditional Indian medicine), the sacred tulsi herb is used in fresh, dried, and powdered form, as well as in tea and essential oil. Tulsi helps ameliorate outside stressors.

My Self-Care Intentions for the Week

BODY ....

MIND ....

SPIRIT ....

week 2

month 5

Week of   /   /

As you schedule your week, keep your self-care intentions in mind.

Sunday

Monday

Tuesday

Wednesday

Thursday

Friday

Saturday

How did I do?

....

....

....

BODY Eat More Walnuts

The walnut and human brain share some similarities—both have two hemispheres and lots of wrinkles. Research shows that eating walnuts is a great way to nourish your brain. Consuming walnuts helps you develop more than three dozen neurotransmitters for brain function.

MIND Chase Your Curiosity

Evolutionary scientists have a term for the curiosity trait— *neoteny*. In evolutionary theory, it means "retention of juvenile characteristics." Your childlike, curious mind has a lifelong capacity to learn new things. Learning new stuff, science says, is excellent for your mind. Take up the violin (the most difficult instrument in the orchestra), learn to read ancient Greek, play 3D chess, or take an online or off-line course in a discipline you'd like to learn more about.

SPIRIT Improve Your Spiritual Wellness

Search for deeper understanding of your spiritual core. Ask and answer questions like, "Who am I? What values matter most to me? What spiritual beliefs do I hold as most important?" Exploring your core beliefs helps promote spiritual wellness.

My Self-Care Intentions for the Week

BODY ....

MIND ....

SPIRIT ....

Week of   /   /

As you schedule your week, keep your self-care intentions in mind.

Sunday

Monday

Tuesday

Wednesday

Thursday

Friday

Saturday

How did I do?

....

....

....

This Week's Tips to Honor Your Body

BODY Enjoy a Cup of Home-Blended Tea

Make your own tea blends using store-bought or homemade cotton tea bags. Blend pesticide-free ingredients like rose hips, mint, citrus peel, chamomile, lemongrass, and loose tea. Use 1 teaspoon of tea-herb blend in 1 cup of water. Take joy in your self-care cuppa.

MIND Read about Subjects That Intrigue You

Stimulating the mind is as important as exercising the body. Love to read about scientific breakthroughs, quilting or gardening techniques, herbal remedies, or gluten-free recipes? Indulge yourself. Devise a self-care practice that includes devouring fascinating information.

SPIRIT Meditate On Primordial Sound

According to raja yoga, several types of sounds predated your birth. As the ascending kundalini energy pierces your chakras, you can hear specific sounds within them. Meditate. Press your fingertips against your ears to shut out other sounds. Listen deeply. Insert your intention to honor your beautiful being.

My Self-Care Intentions for the Week

BODY ....

MIND ....

SPIRIT ....

Week of   /   /

As you schedule your week, keep your self-care intentions in mind.

Sunday

Monday

Tuesday

Wednesday

Thursday

Friday

Saturday

How did I do?

....

....

....

This Week's Tips to Honor Your Body

BODY Care for Your Gut Biome

Proper balance of gut bacteria powers a strong immune system and plays an important role in good health and behavior. Make it a self-care habit to enjoy eating yogurt, especially a type with a wide variety of live bacteria.

MIND Protect Against Dementia

If developing dementia in mid- or later life concerns you, recognize and deal with risk factors, such as type 2 diabetes, high total blood cholesterol, elevated blood pressure, and obesity. Make your mantra: "My healthy body supports my healthy mind."

SPIRIT Practice Inverted Asanas and Forward Bends

Is one of your self-care goals to have a deeper, clearer spiritual experience? Try doing a few inverted asanas and forward bends to increase oxygen and blood flow to your head before sitting in meditation, contemplation, or prayer. You'll shine.

week 5

month 5

My Self-Care Intentions for the Week

BODY ....

MIND ....

SPIRIT ....

Week of   /   /

As you schedule your week, keep your self-care intentions in mind.

Sunday

Monday

Tuesday

Wednesday

Thursday

Friday

Saturday

How did I do?

....

....

....

Add Fun Into Your Life

SUN	MON	TUES
/	/	/
/	/	/
/	/	/
/	/	/
/	/	/

"Do anything, but let it produce joy."

—Walt Whitman, American poet

WED	TH	FRI	SAT
/	/	/	/
/	/	/	/
/	/	/	/
/	/	/	/
/	/	/	/

Add Fun Into Your Life

Many spiritual traditions teach that life isn't meant to be so serious. Remember when you were a child how fun came as naturally as waking up? Enjoying the fun aspects of life should be an integral part of your self-care practice. Begin to see the world with an open mind and expect opportunities to arise for experiencing laughter, joy, and silliness. Do something you've never done before. Seize the moment!

My Self-Care Intentions for the Month

_____

_____

_____

_____

_____

_____

_____

_____

_____

month 6

"Today was good. Today was fun. Tomorrow is another one."

—Dr. Seuss, American children's author and cartoonist

Notes

BODY Release Your Inner Child

Throw off the ropes of routine and set your inner child free. There are many health benefits to having fun, including improved memory and circulation, more restful sleep, better coping skills, and reduced stress levels. Color outside the lines, ride a sled down a snowy hill, take a plunge into a sun-kissed creek, or chase butterflies in a wildflower meadow.

MIND Start the Day with a Playful Mind

Launch yourself into each day with a hefty dose of humor. Read daily jokes and giggle about them throughout your day. Laughter should be part of your self-care regimen. It improves cardiac health, boosts T cells, and promotes a sense of well-being.

SPIRIT Connect with the Air Spirits

As a child, did you have an imaginary friend? Adults tend to relegate such close comrades to the past. But metaphysicians believe in sylphs—air spirits who will help you handle mental and communication tasks. Have fun connecting with them by tuning in to nature. Watch for tiny pinpricks of light or a soft glow in a forest glade. Offer a respectful welcome and ask them ask to carry a message to someone for you. Express your gratitude.

My Self-Care Intentions for the Week

BODY ....

MIND ....

SPIRIT ....

month 6 week 1

Week of   /   /

As you schedule your week, keep your self-care intentions in mind.

Sunday

Monday

Tuesday

Wednesday

Thursday

Friday

Saturday

How did I do?

BODY Orchestrate a Yard Sale

Organize a yard sale and include your friends. Not only will you be doing a little self-care by strengthening your social bonds; you'll also be clearing clutter, as will your friends. Less stuff means less stress, more time, and more money.

MIND Try Turmeric

The active ingredient in turmeric, a spice and medicinal herb used in Ayurveda, is curcumin. Curcumin is an anti-inflammatory and a strong antioxidant, and it boosts a particular brain hormone that increases growth of new neurons. Before taking this powerful herb, check with your doctor.

SPIRIT Join a Kirtan Group

Kirtan, the ancient practice of chanting, is the means to anchor heart and spirit in the moment through music made by many voices. Chanting, like mantra practice, can take you more deeply inward to the Source of your being.

My Self-Care Intentions for the Week

BODY ....

MIND ....

SPIRIT ....

Week of   /   /

As you schedule your week, keep your self-care intentions in mind.

Sunday

Monday

Tuesday

Wednesday

Thursday

Friday

Saturday

How did I do?

BODY Enjoy a Spa Day

Schedule a trip to wine country: book a room, enjoy some wine (red grape skins contain resveratrol, which fights cancer and heart disease), and get a mud bath or seaweed wrap, or indulge in a warm stone massage. Invite a friend.

MIND Contemplate the Moon

Ancient stargazers viewed the moon's appearance in the night sky as symbolizing the Triple Goddess (Maiden, Mother, and Crone). Long linked to the Divine feminine, the moon is associated with birth, life, and death. What does the moon reflect for you?

SPIRIT Align Your Body's Cycle with the Moon

Ayurveda advocates aligning your body with nature's rhythms to increase feminine energy (Shakti). In ancient times, women would release their physical-emotional blockages and toxins through their menses during the new moon's dark night. Align meditations on Shakti with the moon's cycles.

My Self-Care Intentions for the Week

BODY ....

MIND ....

SPIRIT ....

Week of   /   /

As you schedule your week, keep your self-care intentions in mind.

Sunday

Monday

Tuesday

Wednesday

Thursday

Friday

Saturday

How did I do?

....

....

....

BODY Take Up a New Hobby

Hobbies are self-care stress relievers. Engaged in a fun activity, you feel happy, gain confidence, and (for some hobbies) increase your social network and income. Build a website to showcase your hobby or blog about it to share your hobby with others.

MIND Learn to Play a Musical Instrument

Learning to sing or play a musical instrument is an enjoyable self-care activity that rewards you each time you practice. Your brain forges new neural networks and increases your cognitive, verbal, and literacy skills while enhancing spatial reasoning and improving your memory.

SPIRIT Enjoy Music for a Deeper Spiritual Experience

Hearing a bansuri flute, you might reflect on Krishna (the flute-playing Hindu god) or the bhajans (spiritual songs) of Mirabai. Samuel Barber's *Adagio for Strings* might transport your thoughts to lofty realms. Use music created by others to journey inward.

My Self-Care Intentions for the Week

BODY ....

MIND ....

SPIRIT ....

week 4

month 6

Week of   /   /

As you schedule your week, keep your self-care intentions in mind.

Sunday

Monday

Tuesday

Wednesday

Thursday

Friday

Saturday

How did I do?

....

....

....

BODY Visit the Zoo

Trips to the zoo are especially fun when you go solo. Visit your favorite animals. Take the tram ride with views (if offered). Forge connections with nature's creatures while enjoying self-care time in fresh air and sunshine.

MIND Read Poetry to Laugh

The spare, precise language of poetry can make you laugh out loud, heal pain, or ease longing. Each line has space around it, leaving room for you to ponder and personalize the poem's messages. Find a collection that speaks to you.

SPIRIT Create a Self-Care Meditation Ritual

Create a great ritual as a signal to meditate. Light a candle. Ring a small bell, tap a gong with a mallet, or run the ringing stick around a singing bowl. Make that act the start of your spiritual self-care time.

week 5

month 6

My Self-Care Intentions for the Week

BODY ....

MIND ....

SPIRIT ....

Week of   /   /

As you schedule your week, keep your self-care intentions in mind.

Sunday

Monday

Tuesday

Wednesday

Thursday

Friday

Saturday

How did I do?

....

....

....

Connect with Others

SUN	MON	TUES
/	/	/
/	/	/
/	/	/
/	/	/
/	/	/

> *"You can make more friends in two months by becoming interested in other people than you can in two years by trying to get other people interested in you."*

—Dale Carnegie, American writer and lecturer

WED	TH	FRI	SAT
/	/	/	/
/	/	/	/
/	/	/	/
/	/	/	/
/	/	/	/

Connect with Others

We all have a fundamental human need to belong and to feel loved. That being the case, one of the best things you can do for self-care is to regularly connect with others. A study examined in *Psychology Today* explained how social connections strengthen your immune system, enable you to recover from disease faster, and might even increase your longevity. Conversely, individuals living in isolation can suffer declines in physical and psychological health.

My Self-Care Intentions for the Month

_____

_____

_____

_____

_____

_____

_____

_____

month 7

"Love one another but make not a bond of love: let it rather be a moving sea between the shores of your souls."

—Kahlil Gibran, Lebanese-American author and poet

Notes

BODY Use Friendly Body Language

How you say something is often more important than what you say for a positive first impression. Make eye contact. Uncross your arms (or legs, if sitting) to indicate your openness to the other person. Lean in. Listen intently. Speak kindly.

MIND Be Fully Present

Whether the nature of your bond with someone is romantic, friendly, or professional, it is important to tune out the busyness of the world, set aside distractions, and focus fully on the other person. Give them your undivided attention.

SPIRIT Forge Deep Spiritual Connections

Psychics suggest we easily connect with the spirits of those we've known before. When you notice how easy it is to be with someone you've just met, trust your instincts to guide you into deepening the bond you share.

month 7   week 1

My Self-Care Intentions for the Week

BODY ....

MIND ....

SPIRIT ....

Week of   /   /

As you schedule your week, keep your self-care intentions in mind.

Sunday

Monday

Tuesday

Wednesday

Thursday

Friday

Saturday

How did I do?

....

....

....

BODY Join a Group for Qigong in the Park

Qigong is a holistic system that integrates body, mind, and spirit through posture, controlled breathing, and movement. It's an exercise modality for health, and when you do it with others there is the added benefit of expanding your social contacts.

MIND Join a Club for Thinkers Like You

The human brain relative to its body size is large—possibly an evolutionary adaptation for social thinking. As a self-care exercise, read to better understand why your brain is wired for connecting with others. Meet others who enjoy the same intellectual disciplines or subjects that you do.

SPIRIT Visit a Spiritually Charged Holy Place

Take a break and visit a holy place. Make a pilgrimage to where a holy being has been venerated (perhaps for centuries). Experience the environment supercharged with prayers and positive energy. Recharge your spirit as an act of self-care.

My Self-Care Intentions for the Week

BODY ....

MIND ....

SPIRIT ....

Week of   /   /

As you schedule your week, keep your self-care intentions in mind.

Sunday

Monday

Tuesday

Wednesday

Thursday

Friday

Saturday

How did I do?

This Week's Tips to Connect with Others

BODY Connect with Animal Friends

Do you love dogs and cats? Volunteer to help at your local animal shelter. Meet other people who care about animals and want to make a difference in the lives of creatures that need of human assistance and tender loving care.

MIND Reforge an Old Friend Connection

Friendship, according to numerous studies, plays a key role in human health and well-being. Think about reconnecting with an old friend. If you parted on negative terms, consider ways to mend the rift. Make it your self-care activity to reach out.

SPIRIT Join a Like-Minded Spiritual Group

Saints and spiritual leaders have long emphasized the importance of community to reinforce beliefs and provide companionship. If you have not yet found a spiritual group aligned with your beliefs, form one in either the physical or online networking world.

My Self-Care Intentions for the Week

BODY ....

MIND ....

SPIRIT ....

month 7　week 3

Week of   /   /

As you schedule your week, keep your self-care intentions in mind.

Sunday

Monday

Tuesday

Wednesday

Thursday

Friday

Saturday

How did I do?

This Week's Tips to Connect with Others

BODY Take a Class

Consider subjects that interest you and sign up for a class. Attending a class through adult education or your local community college is a great way to learn something new (improves mind-body health) and also make new friends (enhances health and longevity).

MIND Strengthen Your Telepathic Cord

Your intuitive or psychic bond may be strong enough with one or more friends that if you are thinking of them for no apparent reason, they might be tugging on that invisible telepathic cord connecting you both. Reach out again.

SPIRIT Invite Contact from Your Angels

The majority of Americans believe that angels exist and interact with humans. Would you like to connect with your angels? Clap your hands three times and say, "Angels, come." Talk with them, ask questions, and when finished, thank them.

My Self-Care Intentions for the Week

BODY ....

MIND ....

SPIRIT ....

week 4

month 7

Week of   /   /

As you schedule your week, keep your self-care intentions in mind.

Sunday

Monday

Tuesday

Wednesday

Thursday

Friday

Saturday

How did I do?

....

....

....

This Week's Tips to Connect with Others

BODY Create a Community Garden

Do you love to garden? Why not organize an effort to create a community garden? Gardens are wonderful gathering places. In a community garden, you'll share your love of gardening, grow healthy food, and nurture your friendships. Share the bounty.

MIND Dose Yourself with Laughter

Download some stand-up routines of your favorite comedians and enjoy listening to them while you rest in the backyard hammock. Laugh out loud and often. It boosts your immune system, decreases tension and stress, and energizes your body and mind.

SPIRIT Schedule a Weekend Retreat

Take a weekend trip into the mountains, across a prairie, or near water. Book a room at a monastery, a novitiate, or a conference center. Or, reserve a cabin. Expect to join others who, like you, desire to rejuvenate their spirits.

My Self-Care Intentions for the Week

BODY ....

MIND ....

SPIRIT ....

month 7 week 5

Week of   /   /

As you schedule your week, keep your self-care intentions in mind.

Sunday

Monday

Tuesday

Wednesday

Thursday

Friday

Saturday

How did I do?

....

....

....

Know Yourself

SUN	MON	TUES
/	/	/
/	/	/
/	/	/
/	/	/
/	/	/

"One must know oneself. If this does not serve to discover truth, it at least serves as a rule of life, and there is nothing better."

—Blaise Pascal, French philosopher and physicist

WED	TH	FRI	SAT
/	/	/	/
/	/	/	/
/	/	/	/
/	/	/	/
/	/	/	/

Know Yourself

Perhaps the most important knowledge in the world is self-knowledge. We think of ourselves as physical beings, but many spiritual traditions see humans as multidimensional beings. Science teaches that we are energy. Knowledge of self means you can control your life instead of responding to how life acts upon you. Self-awareness means you understand what motivates you and you understand your strengths, weaknesses, beliefs, and emotions. Begin the inward journey to "I am."

My Self-Care Intentions for the Month

_____

_____

_____

_____

_____

_____

_____

_____

"The words 'I am...' are potent words; be careful what you hitch them to."

—A.L. Kitselman, American mathematician, scientist, and psychologist

Notes

BODY Chant to Supercharge Your Chakras

Chakras are energy centers in the ethereal body that correspond to the physical body. Each chakra has a sound associated with it. Find a chart showing the chakras and get to work, harmonizing, balancing, and supercharging these potent centers through chanting.

MIND Take Up the Practice of Yoga

A yoga workout involves both body and mind. It increases self-knowledge while strengthening muscles, focusing thoughts, and relieving tension. Yoga practice will enhance flexibility and burn calories. Although deemed safe for pregnant women, check with your doctor. Do yoga for self-care.

SPIRIT See Yourself As Eternal

Some spiritual traditions teach that we are neither body nor mind. Hinduism's ancient teachings depict your essential nature as Sat Chit Ananda—truth, consciousness, bliss. Seen through that lens, your spirit-soul at its essence is the indescribable, unchanging, eternal reality. Read about the yoga of Sri Chinmoy, Paramahansa Yogananda, Swami Vivekananda, and other yogis who have spent their lives immersed in ancient Hindu spiritual teachings.

My Self-Care Intentions for the Week

BODY ....

MIND ....

SPIRIT ....

week 1

month 8

Week of   /   /

As you schedule your week, keep your self-care intentions in mind.

Sunday

Monday

Tuesday

Wednesday

Thursday

Friday

Saturday

How did I do?

....

....

....

BODY Do What's Best for You

Freedom in life comes from knowing yourself. When you realize that you are important and do not need approval for doing what's best for you, you can schedule time daily to meditate and practice self-introspection, self-awareness, self-compassion, and self-acceptance.

MIND Learn to Let Go

Turn inward and observe your thoughts. When thoughts block deep absorption, let them go. In this way, your inward work of witnessing and releasing can be replicated in life as obstacles come your way. This self-care practice renders self-care knowledge.

SPIRIT Develop Self-Awareness

Knowing yourself helps you develop self-awareness, which deepens as you continue to reflect on who you are. Self-knowledge guides you toward choices that will nurture your life rather than be destructive. Affirm: "I'm making time to know myself."

week 2

month 8

My Self-Care Intentions for the Week

BODY ....

MIND ....

SPIRIT ....

Week of   /   /

As you schedule your week, keep your self-care intentions in mind.

Sunday

Monday

Tuesday

Wednesday

Thursday

Friday

Saturday

How did I do?

BODY Choose to Practice Wu Wei

The Taoist practice of wu wei (the action of non-doing) allows you to do nothing but observe a situation. You can choose not to get involved. You simply observe the drama of life unfolding without needing to affect a particular outcome.

MIND Embrace Buddhist Thinking about Attachment

Buddha taught that suffering wasn't about physical injury or illness but the dissatisfaction of the mind. No matter what you get, the mind yearns for more and better. Self-knowledge helps you understand that material attachment is at the root of mental dissatisfaction. Take notice of how the thoughts in your mind determine your happiness, not what is around you.

SPIRIT Extend Moments of Your Mind Resting in Itself

Upon awakening after a restful nap, you may not know instantly where you are, who you are, or what went before the moment. You just "are," and that's enough until consciousness fills in the blanks. Extend that moment of powerful self-awareness by breathing in and holding on to the memory of "I am," then breathing out, impressing that awareness on your conscious mind.

My Self-Care Intentions for the Week

BODY ....

MIND ....

SPIRIT ....

week 3

month 8

Week of   /   /

As you schedule your week, keep your self-care intentions in mind.

Sunday

Monday

Tuesday

Wednesday

Thursday

Friday

Saturday

How did I do?

BODY Know Your Ayurveda Body Type

Discover which dominant mind-body type in Ayurveda medicine (dosha) fits you. There are only three—vata, pitta, and kapha. Your dosha does not change over your lifetime. Learn the care and feeding of your type as a self-care exercise. Look up Ayurveda and dosha information on a legitimate website or in books written by experts trained in Ayurvedic medicine.

MIND Know Your Emotional Type

Are you analytical and logical? A good listener who is highly sensitive? Do you remain strong and cool-headed in a crisis? Or do you openly and easily share your emotions? Your self-care might focus on understanding and balancing your emotions or lack of them.

SPIRIT Burn Your Favorite Incense

Incense has been used since ancient times for spiritual purposes. Incense can reduce stress, relax the body, open your heart, and calm your spirit. During your quiet self-care period, light a stick of sandalwood, Nag Champa, or frankincense to feel centered.

My Self-Care Intentions for the Week

BODY ....

MIND ....

SPIRIT ....

week 4

month 8

Week of   /   /

As you schedule your week, keep your self-care intentions in mind.

Sunday

Monday

Tuesday

Wednesday

Thursday

Friday

Saturday

How did I do?

....

....

....

BODY Engage in Positive Self-Talk

Pull back when you realize you've taken on the dark energy of a friend's problems. Understand your capacity to compassionately listen to their needs as opposed to being sucked in too deep. Positive self-talk can shift you back into groundedness.

MIND Set Your Mind Free

Your identification with your ego limits the mind's freedom to experience serenity. Your self-care practice might include periods when you let your impulsive and restless mind have free rein until the thought energies finally slow and peace can flow.

SPIRIT See Yourself in Divine Light

Divine light is in you. The ego blocks this realization and holds you in check. Find edification in the teachings of holy ones, past and present. Make an intention to live in tune with and guided by your inner light.

week 5

month 8

My Self-Care Intentions for the Week

BODY ....

MIND ....

SPIRIT ....

Week of   /   /

As you schedule your week, keep your self-care intentions in mind.

Sunday

Monday

Tuesday

Wednesday

Thursday

Friday

Saturday

How did I do?

....

....

....

Cultivate Abundance

SUN	MON	TUES
/	/	/
/	/	/
/	/	/
/	/	/
/	/	/

"Not what we have but what we enjoy constitutes our abundance."

—Epicurus, Greek philosopher

WED	TH	FRI	SAT
/	/	/	/
/	/	/	/
/	/	/	/
/	/	/	/
/	/	/	/

Cultivate Abundance

Abundance is both a state of mind and a state of being. If your thoughts dwell on lack, you'll sink deeper into that. But shift your focus to feeling gratitude for what you already have and notice how quickly change happens. You'll see how easy it is to attract abundance. Don't say, "I can't afford that." Instead ask, "How can I afford that?" Then brainstorm how to make it happen.

My Self-Care Intentions for the Month

_____

_____

_____

_____

_____

_____

_____

_____

"When I started counting my blessings, my whole life turned around."

—Willie Nelson, American musician

Notes

BODY Set Tangible Goals

Start your goal setting with some quiet time to actively imagine what you deeply desire. Get out some blank cards. Write down your goals. List steps you can take to achieve those goals. Keep the cards where you can see them.

MIND Own Abundance in Thought First

When you truly desire something, yoke the belief that you deserve it to your desire to have it. Establish an invisible magnetic attraction to draw the desired thing to you. To strengthen the pull, mentally revisit that desire, belief, and intention.

SPIRIT Recite Affirmations to Attract Abundance

To manifest your desire, you must change habitual negative patterns of thinking or behavior. Create a short, positive statement (affirmation). For example, to attract prosperity, say: "I open myself now to receive prosperity of all kinds flowing to me." Repeat throughout the day.

month 9   week 1

My Self-Care Intentions for the Week

BODY ....

MIND ....

SPIRIT ....

Week of   /   /

As you schedule your week, keep your self-care intentions in mind.

Sunday

Monday

Tuesday

Wednesday

Thursday

Friday

Saturday

How did I do?

This Week's Tips to Cultivate Abundance

BODY Energize Your Heart Chakra

Create abundant well-being in your body by energizing your heart chakra, which is associated with love and compassion. Energize this chakra by placing rose quartz around you, scenting your environment with rose oil, and visualizing green light (dubbed "God's radiance" and reflecting health and abundance) flowing from your heart.

MIND Define and Draw Abundance to Yourself

Does abundance mean wealth, loving relationships, a satisfying career, happiness, stronger feelings of self-worth, spiritual advancement, or a sense of fulfillment? To attract abundance, first define it. Release limited thinking. Seek guidance. Declare your intention to draw abundance to you.

SPIRIT Discover the Abundance of an Inner Life

Your inner world is a mostly uncharted landscape that you could spend a lifetime exploring. Your heart's desires are linked with your quiet mind. Yoked together, they can power up your spiritual journey. Your self-care activity is to become an inner explorer by diving deep into your interior world of silence and noticing what thoughts arise, what images you see, and what bodily sensations you experience.

My Self-Care Intentions for the Week

BODY ....

MIND ....

SPIRIT ....

month 9   week 2

Week of   /   /

As you schedule your week, keep your self-care intentions in mind.

Sunday

Monday

Tuesday

Wednesday

Thursday

Friday

Saturday

How did I do?

....

....

....

BODY Practice Root Chakra Meditation

Root chakra energy flows upward from the earth, empowering you to access courage for survival while also grounding you. Crystal workers recommend wearing red jasper and obsidian as you learn to trust your instincts. Energize the root chakra to attract wealth.

MIND Boost Brain Power with Vitamins

Vitamin A protects brain cells from damage by free radicals. Vitamin B_9 is a water-soluble vitamin that supports cell division, helps block formation of beta-amyloid plaques, and promotes healthy brain function. Self-care includes taking your vitamins for abundant brain power.

SPIRIT Balance Your Crown Chakra

When the crown chakra is balanced and your awareness rests there, you feel abundant peace, bliss of consciousness, and connectedness to all things. If this chakra needs balancing, envision a violet stream of light around the top of your head.

week 3

month 9

My Self-Care Intentions for the Week

BODY ....

MIND ....

SPIRIT ....

Week of   /   /

As you schedule your week, keep your self-care intentions in mind.

Sunday

Monday

Tuesday

Wednesday

Thursday

Friday

Saturday

How did I do?

....

....

....

BODY **Achieve Abundant Bone Health**

Perform high-impact, weight-bearing, and muscle-strengthening exercises to build and maintain bone density and strength. Dance, hike, jump rope, play tennis, climb stairs, or do aerobics. This self-care ritual for abundant health and optimal functioning of the bones can be fun as well as helpful.

MIND **Create an Abundant Mind-Set**

The phrase "abundant mind-set," formulated by Stephen Covey, encapsulates the idea that there is plenty of everything (resources) for everyone to share. There's no lack for someone else because your share is abundant. Change your thinking about abundance to include everyone.

SPIRIT **Stimulate the Wealth Sector of Your Home**

Feng shui (the ancient Chinese art of placement) advocates energizing your home's wealth sector for financial abundance. Stand at your front entrance facing the interior. Walk to the farthest back-left corner. Place a healthy plant there for financial abundance.

My Self-Care Intentions for the Week

BODY ....

MIND ....

SPIRIT ....

week 4

month 9

Week of   /   /

As you schedule your week, keep your self-care intentions in mind.

Sunday

Monday

Tuesday

Wednesday

Thursday

Friday

Saturday

How did I do?

....

....

....

This Week's Tips to Cultivate Abundance

BODY Celebrate Nature's Abundance

When you enter the green space of a natural environment, you move closer to both the natural world and yourself. The point is that it is the natural world that keeps all of us alive and thriving. If there were no plants to eat, water to drink, or clean air to breathe, many living creatures couldn't survive. But with the help of nature's abundance, we can be abundant, with robust health, optimal mental power, and spirits connected to our Source.

MIND Think More Abundantly

The more success, happiness, relationships, and financial abundance and the like that you seek, the more you need to think abundantly. You are always attracting into your life either lack or abundance. Check your thoughts, because what you think about most is what you manifest.

SPIRIT Discover the Entire Universe As Home

Tantra kundalini yoga teaches that at your crown (sahasrara) chakra, your life-force energy (kundalini) merges your limited ego consciousness with unlimited cosmic consciousness. Practice yoga and advance through the chakras to get there.

My Self-Care Intentions for the Week

BODY ....

MIND ....

SPIRIT ....

Week of   /   /

As you schedule your week, keep your self-care intentions in mind.

Sunday

Monday

Tuesday

Wednesday

Thursday

Friday

Saturday

How did I do?

Practice Gratitude

SUN	MON	TUES
/	/	/
/	/	/
/	/	/
/	/	/
/	/	/

"Gratitude is the single most important ingredient to living a successful and fulfilled life."

—Jack Canfield, American motivational speaker and entrepreneur

WED	TH	FRI	SAT
/	/	/	/
/	/	/	/
/	/	/	/
/	/	/	/
/	/	/	/

Practice Gratitude

Science has shown that expressing gratitude for the kindness of others is not only polite but is also an excellent self-care practice. Showing gratitude bestows on you many health benefits. It lowers blood pressure, reduces pain, and decreases depression. But it also increases positive emotions and self-esteem. Showing gratitude boosts your immunoglobulin, helping your immune system fight off viruses. Being grateful is a simple way of caring for your body, mind, and spirit.

My Self-Care Intentions for the Month

_____

_____

_____

_____

_____

_____

_____

_____

month 10

"Gratitude is not only the greatest of virtues, but the parent of all the others."

—Marcus Tullius Cicero, Roman statesman

Notes

BODY Give Your Body a Moment of Gratitude

Not only is gratitude for your body critical to your well-being; it's also extremely important to your success. Gratitude begets gratitude. "Thank you" is easy to say, so say it often in association with your body, which carries you forward into your dreams.

MIND Feel Appreciative Regardless of Showing It

People who wrote letters of gratitude without sending them still exhibited positive changes to their brain's medial prefrontal cortex, the part of the brain associated with decision-making and learning. It's important to feel appreciative even if you take no action.

SPIRIT Make an Offering

Show gratitude by making an offering to your deity or a sacred place that nourishes your spirit. Write a short prayer to your favorite god, goddess, angel, or spirit. Recite affirmations or sacred mantras for the spiritual sustenance you seek.

My Self-Care Intentions for the Week

BODY ....

MIND ....

SPIRIT ....

Week of   /   /

As you schedule your week, keep your self-care intentions in mind.

Sunday

Monday

Tuesday

Wednesday

Thursday

Friday

Saturday

How did I do?

....

....

....

This Week's Tips to Practice Gratitude

BODY Give Thanks for Messages from Your Muscles

Feel gratitude on ache-free days and on days when your muscles ache. Let pain remind you that you possess the miraculous gift of life. Bless your body for the messages it sends so you can give it the attention it needs.

MIND Appreciate Your Intellectual Inquisitiveness

Science shows that curious people are happy. They are always learning new things. Because they seek new knowledge, they have a strong sense of well-being due to the brain chemicals released in response to their mental forays. Express appreciation for your curious mind.

SPIRIT Go Where Your Spirit Moves You

When you give it permission, where does your spirit lead you? Just as your mind may be inquisitive and curious, your spiritual nature might be communicating something as well. Observe what shows up in your life. Be grateful for how your spirit moves you.

My Self-Care Intentions for the Week

BODY ....

MIND ....

SPIRIT ....

month 10 week 2

Week of   /   /

As you schedule your week, keep your self-care intentions in mind.

Sunday

Monday

Tuesday

Wednesday

Thursday

Friday

Saturday

How did I do?

BODY Be Grateful for Simple Habits

Successful people often credit simple habits done daily as contributing to their high performance. If you practice simple habits like reading, meditating, taking time to breathe, and promoting what you love, be grateful. Do more. Good habits drive excellence.

MIND Thank the Universe for Dealing with Details

A cell in your body doesn't require you to instruct it through the six million or so tasks it performs each second. Give thanks for the freedom to deal with intentions for your life while the Universe organizes the details.

SPIRIT The Space Between Thoughts Deserves Gratitude

The most powerful thing you need to be aware of is the space between your thoughts. Dive deeply into meditation. Discern that space. Then gently insert your deepest desire for it to become reality. Your self-care act is to appreciate that gift.

My Self-Care Intentions for the Week

BODY ....

MIND ....

SPIRIT ....

Week of   /   /

As you schedule your week, keep your self-care intentions in mind.

Sunday

Monday

Tuesday

Wednesday

Thursday

Friday

Saturday

How did I do?

BODY Feel Gratitude for Your Eyes

High in vitamin C, raw bell peppers are good for the blood vessels in your eyes and may thwart cataracts. Almonds slow macular degeneration. For vision, eat dark, leafy greens (rich in vitamins C and E) and give thanks for your eyesight.

MIND Appreciate Your Mental Ability

Enjoy playing Go, concentrating on chess, or doing the Sunday crossword puzzle? Whichever mental pastime is to your liking, show some love and gratitude for the able mind that makes your enjoyment possible. For self-care, have fun and be grateful.

SPIRIT Find Gratitude for What's Hidden in Each Moment

What comes in each moment serves your personal evolution. You might not like this moment, the people in it, or the circumstances. Change the future, but for now accept and appreciate this moment as perfect because of what's hidden in it.

My Self-Care Intentions for the Week

BODY ....

MIND ....

SPIRIT ....

Week of   /   /

As you schedule your week, keep your self-care intentions in mind.

Sunday

Monday

Tuesday

Wednesday

Thursday

Friday

Saturday

How did I do?

This Week's Tips to Practice Gratitude

BODY Be Thankful for Your Hands

Think of all the ways you use your hands each day. Two hands can cradle an infant, feed the hungry, comfort a sick person, fold blankets for the homeless, or cook a meal for forty at summer camp. Feel gratitude for your hands.

MIND Create a Gratitude Journal

Gratitude pulls your mental focus into the present and improves your happiness, health, and well-being. Write answers to these questions in your journal: "Today, what am I grateful for? What inspires me, gives me comfort, and brings me peace?"

SPIRIT Give Thanks When You Worship

Regardless of the moniker you use to address the higher power in your life, remember to be thankful for the gifts of Spirit. Each time you sit for meditation or prayer, offer praise and gratitude in remembrance of your higher power.

My Self-Care Intentions for the Week

BODY ....

MIND ....

SPIRIT ....

Week of   /   /

As you schedule your week, keep your self-care intentions in mind.

Sunday

Monday

Tuesday

Wednesday

Thursday

Friday

Saturday

How did I do?

....

....

....

Set Limits

SUN	MON	TUES
/	/	/
/	/	/
/	/	/
/	/	/
/	/	/

month 11

"Conquering any difficulty always gives one a secret joy, for it means pushing back a boundary-line and adding to one's liberty."

—Henri-Frederic Amiel, Swiss moral philosopher and critic

WED	TH	FRI	SAT
/	/	/	/
/	/	/	/
/	/	/	/
/	/	/	/
/	/	/	/

Set Limits

Many of us struggle for equilibrium in our overscheduled lives. Juggling work with family life and personal time, we might not even realize how we've tipped out of balance. The transitions are perhaps most noticeable during seasonal shifts (for example: from unhurried summer days to hectic fall schedules or from quiet winter pursuits to busy spring activities). This month, try to slow the pace, establish personal boundaries, and set limits on work and family demands.

My Self-Care Intentions for the Month

_____

_____

_____

_____

_____

_____

_____

_____

_____

month 11

"The difference between successful people and really successful people is that really successful people say 'No' to almost everything."

—Warren Buffett, American business magnate

Notes

This Week's Tips to Set Limits

BODY Slow the Roll

Doing things faster won't accomplish more. Instead, assess your daily activities to determine what can reasonably be achieved. Try limiting the work you take on each day. Slow down and do your tasks with focus, making each activity as important as the next.

MIND Limit Monkey-Mind Thinking

A busy mind thwarts focus. If racing thoughts drive your stress levels higher, limit that mental activity through breath work. Let your belly rise as you inhale to the count of three; let it fall to the count of seven as you exhale.

SPIRIT Establish a Boundary for Inner Work

Your deepest need each day is to limit outward pursuits and dive inward. Which tasks can you move to the next day for a reprieve from work and family obligations? Enter solitude. Feel welcomed by your spirit. Commune, refresh, and recharge.

month 11   week 1

My Self-Care Intentions for the Week

BODY ....

MIND ....

SPIRIT ....

Week of   /   /

As you schedule your week, keep your self-care intentions in mind.

_____

Sunday

_____

Monday

_____

Tuesday

_____

Wednesday

_____

Thursday

_____

Friday

_____

Saturday

How did I do?

....

....

....

This Week's Tips to Set Limits

BODY Be Patient with Your Body

Ignore the "no pain, no gain" adage and instead, honor the wisdom of your body as you exercise. Know where your limits are and how vigorously to push against them. Improving your workout is good. Hurting yourself in the process is not.

MIND Establish Limits in Romantic Relationships

Your romantic self-care can take the role of speaking honestly about your rules and personal boundaries. Encourage your romantic partner to be forthcoming as well. A lot of relationships break up because limits are unclear, and unspoken boundaries are violated.

SPIRIT Rely On Your Higher Self

The spark of the Divine dwells within you (your higher self). Therein is your power to manifest whatever you desire for your life, keeping something out or drawing something in. Remember and recite this affirmation: "All I need is right here within me."

My Self-Care Intentions for the Week

BODY ....

MIND ....

SPIRIT ....

Week of   /   /

As you schedule your week, keep your self-care intentions in mind.

Sunday

Monday

Tuesday

Wednesday

Thursday

Friday

Saturday

How did I do?

....

....

....

BODY Limit Long Periods of Sitting

Your day job might require you to be desk-bound all day. If so, your self-care practice should include frequent standing and stretching, walking during lunch, or doing yoga poses during coffee breaks. Even small movements counteract the negative effects of being sedentary.

MIND Limit Screen Time

Staring at a computer screen without letup is unhealthy—it can cause eye strain, mental fatigue, blurred vision, and headaches. The University of Illinois recommends breaks every hour for five to ten minutes. Use breaks to move and alleviate your aching shoulders, neck, and back.

SPIRIT Mute Outer Voices to Hear the Inner One

There's no dearth of voices today ready to tell you to follow them to reach the proverbial spiritual mountaintop. Meditate to shut out those voices and pay attention to your own. Ask, "What do I need to support my spiritual practice?" Listen deeply for the answer.

week 3

month 11

My Self-Care Intentions for the Week

BODY ....

MIND ....

SPIRIT ....

Week of   /   /

As you schedule your week, keep your self-care intentions in mind.

Sunday

Monday

Tuesday

Wednesday

Thursday

Friday

Saturday

How did I do?

BODY Limit High-Calorie, Low-Nutrition Foods

When cooked without fats like butter and cheese, potatoes are healthy to eat, but you should limit French fries and potato chips. Also cut down on white bread, candy bars, sugary drinks, and high-calorie coffee concoctions. For a simple self-care strategy, forgo fruit juices and choose real fruit.

MIND Limit Self-Focus on Aches and Pains

Minor aches and pains are prevalent in a busy life. Try to not obsess over them so that your day is consumed with negative thinking. Enjoy flexibility exercises, a healthy diet, and holistic treatments. If your discomfort worsens, see a doctor.

SPIRIT Practice Mouna (Vow of Silence)

Abstain from speaking and other means of communication. Start for ten to fifteen minutes. You will develop willpower, limit impulsive speech, and curb tendencies of thought chatter. You will learn to speak more thoughtfully and listen more carefully. You'll experience peace.

week 4

month 11

My Self-Care Intentions for the Week

BODY ....

MIND ....

SPIRIT ....

Week of   /   /

As you schedule your week, keep your self-care intentions in mind.

Sunday

Monday

Tuesday

Wednesday

Thursday

Friday

Saturday

How did I do?

....

....

....

BODY Set Limits on Endurance

Pay close attention to the signals your body sends when you are doing exercise or yard work or tasks at your job. Pushing beyond boundaries of endurance can cause damage and pain. Accept that your body knows when it's reached a limit.

MIND Lessen Pain Using Your Mind

Harvard Medical School notes that it's possible to limit the need for pain medication through guided imagery, relaxation, meditation, and positive thinking. Although the brains of long-term pain sufferers send pain signals even after pain is gone, mind-body therapies can help.

SPIRIT Conquer Yourself

Gautama Buddha taught that "Greater in battle than the man who would conquer a thousand-thousand men, is he who would conquer just one—himself." Limit contact with adversaries who squabble and fight. Instead, focus on what you can conquer within.

My Self-Care Intentions for the Week

BODY ....

MIND ....

SPIRIT ....

month 11   week 5

Week of   /   /

As you schedule your week, keep your self-care intentions in mind.

Sunday

Monday

Tuesday

Wednesday

Thursday

Friday

Saturday

How did I do?

....

....

....

Improve Your World

SUN	MON	TUES
/	/	/
/	/	/
/	/	/
/	/	/
/	/	/

*"How wonderful it is that nobody need wait a single moment
before starting to improve the world."*

—Anne Frank, German-Jewish author

WED	TH	FRI	SAT
/	/	/	/
/	/	/	/
/	/	/	/
/	/	/	/
/	/	/	/

Improve Your World

The world needs its citizens to protect and care for it. Start with the attitude that a better world begins with a better you. Consider how your self-care practices can benefit all the world's inhabitants. Choose your words carefully. Speak gently. Volunteer, drive less, walk more, and waste less food or grow your own food and share it with your community food bank. Help whenever and wherever you can.

My Self-Care Intentions for the Month

_____

_____

_____

_____

_____

_____

_____

_____

"We are what we think...with our thoughts, we make the world."

—Gautama Buddha, founder of Buddhism

Notes

This Week's Tips to Improve Your World

BODY Praise Someone Every Day

Praise is a great way to open a conversation with everyone you meet. Speak truthfully from your heart and watch how your action generates a responding feeling of goodwill—a win-win for you and the wider world.

MIND Meditate with Others

During 1987's Harmonic Convergence, the planets aligned in a spectacular way, and people meditated alone or in groups around the globe to bring about world peace. Join a group meditation. The highly charged atmosphere can make you feel relaxed, uplifted, and peaceful.

SPIRIT Empower People Around You

Stand as a spiritual exemplar of positive change through self-care practices. Help others see how negative thinking can block the life they've always dreamed of having. Empower others to see that they, too, can be catalysts for positive change. Start by offering positive alternative statements to someone's criticisms of self and others.

My Self-Care Intentions for the Week

BODY ....

MIND ....

SPIRIT ....

month 12   week 1

Week of   /   /

As you schedule your week, keep your self-care intentions in mind.

Sunday

Monday

Tuesday

Wednesday

Thursday

Friday

Saturday

How did I do?

BODY Make Someone Happy

Show respect for someone's humanity with a smile. Compliment a worker at the bank, gas station, or post office. Embark on a weekly visit to a nearby nursing home. Smile and make eye contact with a homeless person.

MIND Vote with Your Conscience

Too many Americans who have the right to vote often don't. You can make a difference in your community, state, and nation by making a commitment to study the issues, choose a candidate whom you believe in, and go vote.

SPIRIT Meditate On World Peace

Armed conflicts exert a costly toll on human life. Those fighting risk life and limb. Families with children, fleeing the violence, are displaced and demoralized. Focus your meditation on the end of these conflicts and for peace to reign supreme upon our planet for people of all nations.

month 12   week 2

My Self-Care Intentions for the Week

BODY ....

MIND ....

SPIRIT ....

Week of   /   /

As you schedule your week, keep your self-care intentions in mind.

Sunday

Monday

Tuesday

Wednesday

Thursday

Friday

Saturday

How did I do?

....

....

....

This Week's Tips to Improve Your World

BODY Move Your Body for Activism

Choose your cause. Show your support. Get out and mobilize. Use your contacts and social media platforms to find like-minded followers who support your cause, whether it deals with medicine, politics, women's rights, human rights, or feeding children. Make your beliefs known.

MIND Make a Difference in a Child's Life

Become a mentor. Teach a teen a life skill, like how to balance a checkbook, save and invest money, or understand how to calculate interest on loans. Donate a backpack of classroom supplies to your local school. Better still, organize a drive.

SPIRIT Join a Spiritual Community

Consider joining a spiritual community that aligns with your spiritual beliefs. Get involved in the group's work to make the world a better place for all of us. Already involved? Establish a new chapter to expand the work, perhaps in a new direction.

My Self-Care Intentions for the Week

BODY ....

MIND ....

SPIRIT ....

month 12 week 3

Week of   /   /

As you schedule your week, keep your self-care intentions in mind.

Sunday

Monday

Tuesday

Wednesday

Thursday

Friday

Saturday

How did I do?

BODY Be an Exemplar of Respect

Show the world what respect looks like. Watch your language and your tone. Relinquish your subway seat to a senior citizen or a pregnant woman. Share your taxi. When you see a need, offer your help. Be gracious about it.

MIND Learn about Different Cultures

Take time to learn about the customs, history, and social conventions of people in countries you visit on vacation or meet through business. Learning new information can help you navigate most cultural divides. Travel, enjoy local conviviality, and learn.

SPIRIT Plant Seeds for Your Future

According to practitioners of the Law of Attraction, your present thoughts determine your future. Mentally enter the sanctuary of your heart. Train your thoughts on attracting a kinder, greener, more equally prosperous and peaceful world for us all.

month 12   week 4

My Self-Care Intentions for the Week

BODY ....

MIND ....

SPIRIT ....

Week of   /   /

As you schedule your week, keep your self-care intentions in mind.

Sunday

Monday

Tuesday

Wednesday

Thursday

Friday

Saturday

How did I do?

....

....

....

BODY Teach Your Children to Lead

Teach your children the rules for home and school that must be obeyed and explain why. Rehearse these rules with them. Encourage their development of successful behaviors for relationships they have in sports and other enrichment activities. Help them feel confident.

MIND Develop a Diverse Circle of Support

You have better mental and physical health when you enjoy regular social activities with others, according to a MacArthur Foundation study on aging. The benefits increase with diversity. Welcome people with different religious, racial, or socioeconomic backgrounds, or who hold different political beliefs than you do.

SPIRIT Be a Light-Bearer

It's been said that the light from a single lamp can lift us all. Imagine that together, we are reflecting our light and dispelling darkness from the world. Let us all, in this millennium, usher in lasting peace and prosperity.

My Self-Care Intentions for the Week

BODY ....

MIND ....

SPIRIT ....

week 5

month 12

Week of   /   /

As you schedule your week, keep your self-care intentions in mind.

Sunday

Monday

Tuesday

Wednesday

Thursday

Friday

Saturday

How did I do?

....

....

....